C000221642

I AM A WOMAN

WOMAN

BUT I AM NOT

DUMB

101 ACTIONS OF A WISE WOMAN

Published by Mattyson Media an imprint of MAMM
Matthew Ashimolowo Media Ministries
57 Waterden Road
Hackney Wick
London
E15 2EE

Bible quotes are from the King James Bible
unless otherwise stated.
ISBN 1 874 646-34-1

Printed in Great Britain by
Clays Ltd, St Ives plc

They do not get into foolish courtships.

Courtship times are the times of discovery, they are the times of determination. Courtship times are the days when you seek God's direction. It should not be a time you expect all your previous wounds to be healed. Do not allow the man to become the centre of your life during courtship times, and also in marriage. You leave that to Jesus.

Courtship times should not be controlling you, it is better to ride a lonely period and come out strong. You would be into foolish courtship if you are after a person purely because he is a father figure. You would be into foolish courtship if you hang around the person who abuses you emotionally, sexually, physically or verbally.

They do not get into emotional attachments.

Be ye not unequally yoked together with unbelievers: for what fellowship hath righteousness with unrighteousness? and what communion hath light with darkness?
And what concord hath Christ with Belial? or what part hath he that believeth with an infidel?
And what agreement hath the temple of God with idols? for ye are the temple of the living God; as God hath said, I will dwell in them, and walk in them; and I will be their God, and they shall be my people.
Wherefore come out from among them, and be ye separate, saith the Lord, and touch not the unclean thing; and I will receive you,
And will be a Father unto you, and ye shall be my sons and daughters, saith the Lord Almighty.
2 Corinthians 6:14-18 (KJV)

You may have waited so long for a man to come into your life, but that does not mean you have to put up with "bad news". If you do that you might just be holding onto a person who is 'commitment phobic'. He has promised several ladies without using a word that commits him to any relationship.

When we become unnecessarily attached to certain people or places they may turn around and burn us.

6

Because you have gone through some hurts in your past does not mean that yesterday's hurt should make you take whatever comes.

Even when it is clear that there is no future to a relationship, some people still hold on. Be wise, look for something to direct your time and energy into and stop running after love.

A man would always rise to the level you present to him. Make yourself deserving to receive affection. Make yourself deserving to feel and give affection. Stop sacrificing your destiny to prove to the man that you love him, you might be loving without being loved.

It is not wise to stop and give up your dream because you want to make a relationship happen, rather let him prove that he deserves your hand by making your dream happen.

They do not get into foolish attachments.

*Be ye not unequally yoked together with unbelievers: for what
fellowship hath righteousness with unrighteousness? and what
communion hath light with darkness?
And what concord hath Christ with Belial? or what part hath
he that believeth with an infidel?
And what agreement hath the temple of God with idols? for
ye are the temple of the living God; as God hath said, I will
dwell in them, and walk in them; and I will be their God, and
they shall be my people.
Wherefore come out from among them, and be ye
separate, saith the Lord, and touch not the unclean thing;
and I will receive you,
And will be a Father unto you, and ye shall be my sons and
daughters, saith the Lord Almighty.
2 Corinthians 6:14-18 (KJV)*

Getting into foolish attachments may make you lose
your self value. It is better not to be in any
relationship than to be in a bad one.

Because you want to be in a relationship does not
mean you should become enslaved. A bad
relationship may be a sign that it is time to break
away from uncomfortable contacts.

You need to stop selling yourself. The man who you are courting should want you for who you are without you going out of the way to impress him. Stop working hard just to be accepted.

It is unwise for a woman to give the impression of "I cannot be without you". You need to break away from the ideal emotional relationship you desire, if you do not, you might be falling in love with yourself and living in denial.

A lady who is foolishly attached will accept abuse in courtship; physical, emotional and otherwise. She would hold on despite the spiritual state of the relationship, even where everything seems to indicate that it is time to jump out.

Foolish attachment sometimes is an indication that a person is trying to replace a lost friend, a lost father or partner. Foolish attachment may be a case of holding on because of previous delays. Those in foolish attachment may be in the relationship but really alone.

They do not get foolishly passionate.

But if they cannot contain, let them marry: for it is better to marry than to burn.
1 Corinthians 7:9 (KJV)

Passion and emotion is a blessing from God with which we express ourselves to the opposite sex and within the context of scripture and the will of God, to our spouse.

This applies to both the single and the married. For the single the remembrance must always be there that one night of heaven can wake you up in hell and the consequences of sex outside marriage may be that of a lifelong hurt.

For the woman who is married, passion with wisdom is to not have to remind him of how long there has been romance. It is not being the first to talk about feelings. Passion, for the married woman is not having to always be the first to give a hug. Not having to be the one to grab the hand of your partner all the time, or make sexual advances to him. Passion with wisdom is not being the one to always move to his side of the bed, and not always the first to move to make up when there is a disagreement.

Yes it is your marriage, but if you keep sending him cards when he offends you, you might end up in an abusive relationship.

Passion with wisdom is not being the one to always create the romantic atmosphere, not being the one who does all the talking. It is not covering up when he is not responding. You should not be romancing the marriage for both of you, it must be a dual investment.

Being foolishly passionate is to be lying to yourself that the relationship is great when you are being loving without being loved.

They do not get into the "living together" thing.

Marriage is honourable in all, and the bed undefiled: but whoremongers and adulterers God will judge.
Hebrews 13:4 (KJV)

At these times when libertinian philosophies of "if it feels good, do it" has taken over our society, the scriptures cannot be broken. God's Word still stands on matters of cohabitation. The Bible calls living together a sin, and when you live together in sin, it blocks your spiritual, emotional and marital maturity. Statistics have shown us that cohabiting couples are more likely to divorce faster than those who never lived together before their wedding night.

When you live together you erode the foundation of a good future, and walk in complete opposition to the revealed will of God. You cannot defile the bed of your marriage and question the infidelity of your spouse. You sowed the seed, and the harvest will follow. Ninety percent of common-law marriages fail because they have opened their Christmas gift before Christmas. If the man loves enough, he should lead the woman to the altar.

They do not get into unwise submission.

Know ye not, that to whom ye yield yourselves servants to obey, his servants ye are to whom ye obey; whether of sin unto death, or of obedience unto righteousness?
Romans 6:16 (KJV)

Ephesians 5:24 enjoins the woman to submit to her husband, but this is clearly who, according to verse 18 is in submission himself to the Holy Spirit,

Therefore as the church is subject unto Christ, so let the wives be to their own husbands in every thing.
Ephesians 5:24 (KJV)

And be not drunk with wine, wherein is excess; but be filled with the Spirit;
Ephesians 5:18 (KJV)

and because of his commitment to the will of God through the Holy Spirit, what he will suggest and bring across to his wife will be in agreement with the revealed will of God. Foolish submission on the other hand exposes a woman to abuse.

It is foolish submission when you act as if you must earn your spouse's love, you are being unwise if you are working hard to be loved. Foolish submission makes you to express love that is born out of fear of things falling apart. It makes you to make excuses for the inexcusable, and the very act of foolish submission will make a woman fall apart.

You need to recognise as a woman that you have a desire to always fill gaps. A woman cannot stand an empty locker, she has to fill it with something. She cannot stand silence, there has to be talking. Everyone must be doing something, there has to be activity going on.

Do not fill his inactivity with your own action; do not fill his separation with your love. You should be in submission but it is only to those things that honour God. Ask yourself and list what ways the Bible teaches you to submit. Let him know you expect him to talk, and let him love you tenderly.

In a truly enjoyable relationship, you should be able to tell your spouse to surprise you, because if you wait, your spouse may not. If you tell your spouse to surprise you, to challenge you he might rise to the occasion.

Standing on your own feet emotionally will show you whether your spouse has been involved or interested in the marriage or not, but foolish submission will make a person think that the gap is being filled while they are the ones filling it.

They avoid having babies for the wrong reasons.

Lo, children are an heritage of the LORD: and the fruit of the womb is his reward.
As arrows are in the hand of a mighty man; so are children of the youth.
Happy is the man that hath his quiver full of them: they shall not be ashamed, but they shall speak with the enemies in the gate.
Psalms 127:3-5 (KJV)

Children are the heritage of the Lord, they are a gift from God and we are commanded to replenish the earth. Women look forward to be able to hold within their arms the wonderful gift of children. But proper parenthood will put a child's need first, and therefore will make a woman to avoid what is called an "accidental pregnancy".

To seek for babies in order to get the man to marry you; to seek for babies in order to get a government to be more responsive to you in certain settings; to seek for babies in order to fill a gap in your life will be bringing another human being to this world for the wrong reasons.

A bastard shall not enter into the congregation of the LORD;
even to his tenth generation shall he not enter into the
congregation of the LORD.
Deuteronomy 23:2 (KJV)

It is foolish to yank commitment from a man
using pregnancy. God wants you to have children,
but they should be for signs and wonders. And if
somebody wants you to have a sexual relationship
with them, the fear of having babies should not just
be why you say no. The safest sex control out of
wedlock is "no sex please, I'm a godly woman".

They do not have foolish expectations.

Certain challenges in life leave us with dysfunctions, but when we get to the point where we are considering sharing our life with persons of the opposite sex, we must be wise and godly enough to ensure that our reasons are based on God's Word.

If you get into foolish expectations, you might be marrying a man to cover your childhood hurts. You might be running around a man just because he is all you can find.

It is wise not to court a guy whom you thought would build your self-esteem. He possibly may be used of God to do that, but it should not be your primary reason for courting him. Do not submit to his expectations of you doing things like you are married.

They avoid the "I can't help it" syndrome.

Men and women handle emotions differently. While a woman processes information firstly with the right side of her brain, the side of emotion and later with the left, the side of logic. A man starts with logic first and then emotion, and may not properly handle his emotions like a woman will.

The way you behave around a man determines what comes out of him. If you raise a godly standard, he will come up to your standard. Let the man relate to you emotionally without giving him the attitude of "deserve me". Allow the godly anger that will make you say "never again" when you are tempted to walk out of the will of God.

Shake yourself out of self-blame if the brother is doing what you know is unhealthy for you and your relationship with God. Do not allow yourself to be carried away on a guilt trip that may make you succumb to what does not glorify God.

They do not get into "foolish holding on".

Several stories come across to you on women who hold on in spite of abuse, and you wonder what is she still looking for in him. You are particularly disturbed because you know she knows that he is unfaithful; possibly addicted to something; and insensitive to her, and moreover he controls her and her children.

Some people stay in abusive relationships for different reasons: for the kids; some because they do not want a one-parent situation; others because it brings financial security; or in some situations the fear of a worse experience. Age concern becomes a reason if people have waited for so long. Sometimes in the face of obvious abuse, a lot are ready to go on. Particularly when the man uses their weakness as a bait.

But the worst "foolish holding on", is to hold on to the thought that one day a married man who is probably happy with his spouse will leave her for you, that is a "foolish holding on". Let go!

They do not lower their standard and sell themselves short.

I hate them with perfect hatred: I count them mine enemies.
Psalms 139:22 (KJV)

Why would a woman sell herself short when she only has one life? There are several reasons why people do that. Sometimes it is because of the feeling that this might be their last chance, or falling prey to the "everyone is doing it" trap. Do not fall into the trap, do not fall into all the lies that are around.

Sexual impurity is the number one trap that Satan will set before you whether you like it or not. It may come from a person you regard and respect, and even know to be a Christian, and he makes the statement "if you love me, sleep with me" or "that's not what Pastor meant", "let's get married quick, I can't wait to have sex".

While sex may be one major reason for you to get married, it is not enough a reason to rush to the altar. Sex is not something you supply, but what you share in marriage. And if you cannot find a man who can honour you and hold on until the right day, or the proper time, then you may be in trouble. You need to pray for the man who would wait until tomorrow if you are not in the mood, and if he can not control his appetite when he is single, he will have difficulty even in marriage.

They do not cheapen themselves.

Scarcity makes a commodity expensive, rarity increases the price of a thing. Where there is an over supply, price falls.

There is only one YOU! The blood that bought you is too precious, that is why you should raise the standard of the life you live. There is only one you, that is why whoever should have your hand, should truly deserve it.

Where people cheapen themselves; they pick anything that comes by the wayside. Wise women know their worth and value from the point of scriptures.

According as his divine power hath given unto us all things that pertain unto life and godliness, through the knowledge of him that hath called us to glory and virtue:
Whereby are given unto us exceeding great and precious promises: that by these ye might be partakers of the divine nature, having escaped the corruption that is in the world through lust.
2 Peter 1:3-4 (KJV)

They do not dress to seduce

And, behold, there met him a woman with the attire of an harlot, and subtil of heart.
Proverbs 7:10 (KJV)

Clothings are supposed to be primarily to cover nakedness, as social beings to express our beauty, to relate to our world and be acceptable to those around us.

When the man you are married to, or the man you go out with begins to suggest clothes that are indecent, there may be other problems behind it.

It is a sign of danger when your man wants your skirt shorter, it is dangerous when he wants your blouses tighter, when he prefers you in skin tight jeans and micro minis. It is not helpful when he is turning you to a plaything.

You must be wise enough to refuse the "come and get me" clothes. The man who cannot say I love you when you are in old sweaters is dangerous. Men who prefer suggestive clothings are actually fulfilling a fantasy through you.

Contrary to what many women think, there are men, and they are in the majority, who are rather attracted to strength and beauty, not vulgarity and that which is suggestive.

Go out there and enhance your beauty, portray the strength which God has put in you. Show decorum, be attractive. Attraction and attention are not the same thing.

They do not walk in self pity.

Let the redeemed of the LORD say so, whom he hath
redeemed from the hand of the enemy;
Psalms 107:2 (KJV)

Self pity is one of the worst enemies of a woman in waiting. It is such a challenge particulary in a world that is so full of dysfunctions and disappointments. Nonetheless, if you walk in self-pity you will sell yourself to the lowest bidder.

A woman who walks in self pity will see men as a band-aid to all problems. She will carry herself as a victim not a victor. She will think if she kisses a toad, he will turn to a prince.

A woman who walks in self-pity will deny, ignore, rationalise, justify, and keep saying "I love him, in spite of his addictions, weakness, and horrible ways of treating me".

A woman who walks in self-pity has brought herself low, and is likely to pick an abuser. They think they will find someone who will tolerate them because they feel bad in themselves. They comfort themselves by feeling that half a loaf is better than none.

Women who walk in self-pity are particularly age conscious, they believe that this is their last chance, so they try to run away from reality by helping the man they have found.

Before you do, they would as a matter of fact list all the weaknesses the man has. They will start with "I know he's abusive, mean, cold, uncommunicative, negative. I know he's a bully, violent, addicted, controlling, a workaholic, jealous" and end it with "but I love him."

They think yesterday's hurt should mean today's cowardice.

A wise woman should use the Word to build her self-esteem until people give her the due respect, admiration, appreciation, affection, co-operation, and honour.

They refuse to use their sexuality to control men.

That they may teach the young women to be sober, to love their husbands, to love their children,
To be discreet, chaste, keepers at home, good, obedient to their own husbands, that the word of God be not blasphemed.
Titus 2:4-5 (KJV)

Men by nature have to be attracted to the opposite sex, that is the way they were made, so are women. Men by nature also are easily swayed by the sexuality of a woman they meet. Men who know Christ and walk in the will of God are themselves first attracted to a woman's spirituality, without denigrating her sexually.

A godly wise woman knows she must not use her sensuality to control the men around her, because she might be sending out the wrong message. Fishing in the wrong waters, will make you end up with piranahs and other dangerous fishes.

If you are married, using your sexuality to control your spouse, you will be relegating the marriage bed to that similar to prostitution where people pay to get what they want.

They do not stay in relationships out of pity and sorrow for a man.

For as many as are led by the Spirit of God, they are the sons of God.
Romans 8:14 (KJV)

A woman by nature is turned on by competence, particularly in a man. A relationship is destined for disaster if it is premised upon pity for the man. The less achieving a man is, the unhappier you will be as a woman. You will be tempted to talk down at him, this will further complicate things because a woman's words can both open and shut a man down. A man can be inspired or feel expired purely by the words of his wife.

There is danger if he does not want to open up, if he has a chronic need to be controlled; there is danger if a man does not participate in seeking help for himself, he keeps on giving excuses for his behaviours. There is danger, if he does not want to overcome his self destructive addictions,and is playing the blame game.

29

There is danger if his attitude to life is hopelessly negative.

So, you might be faced with a man who has a lot of guilt, self-blame and poor self-esteem based on the past. You will do everything for him if you stay in that relationship purely out of self-pity.

A woman must not leave a relationship because a man is less achieving, but must not stay in it because the man sees her as his emotional crutch.

Wise women maintain their godly, unique identity.

Some women have found themselves in relationships where they are totally overwhelmed and absorbed into the personality, programme, and perspective of the person they have married. They lose everything to the man and live in his shadows for the rest of their life.

It is not wrong if a man has a destiny to pursue and you are standing by your man. The woman must be ready to make sacrifices to make a vision happen, but within your spouse's vision and dream, you should find fulfilment for your talent, dream, interest or career.

They do not cut all other contacts for a man.

The scriptures say a man and woman shall become one flesh as they leave and cleave. There is one extremity where some having left, have not totally departed from home, they get all orders from home.

There is also the other end of the pendulum where some people leave, and their spouses would not allow even the simplest of contacts with other people.

If you find yourself in this predicament, doing so is giving up part of yourself. If you are sacrificing all of your desires, dreams, visions and goals to be accepted by a man, there will very soon be nothing of you left.

If this man leaves, you will start the journey of looking for the next person. After four courtships you will be totally unrecognisable.

The man may disapprove of your relations because they can see through him, he may feel insecure around them, and insecure men always make demands that those who expose them should be cut off.

Avoiding the danger of being moulded into what he wanted is necessary for you, because if the relationship ends who would you call?

Your relations love you not for what you could give but because you are part of them. A woman should remember who made them somebody. You should also remember girls who made somebody's dream come true, and after his dream was fulfilled he dumped them.

It is great to sacrifice for a man, it is wrong when it is one-sided. When you are busy working hard to make someone love you, you lose your self-love. You must not assume that a man's actions means what it might not.

They do not fall for a man's status.

A man's status is a product of achievement, it can come and go. Women by nature are attracted to those who are achievers. But always remember that the primary person to fall in love with is the man himself and not what he is within his status. If you fall in love with his status, you may fall out of love the day he loses his status.

If you court a man because he is for example in parliament, what would be your fate the day he is out and probably even chooses to live in a remote unknown village?

They do not fall for a man's future ability.

It is great to be attracted to a man's future potential, but it is very important to accept him for what he is now, and not try to make of him what you think he should be.

A woman must not run after a man because he is for example a doctor. Suppose he is incapable of making you happy. Many women have fallen for the promise of the man to change, or they have asked the man to change, and then when he changed they did not like the outcome.

Leave a man alone to love himself enough to want to change than to make attempts to make him what you want him to be.

True romance is to be happy with who he is now, not what he will be in the future. The consequence of making a man become what you want him to be is a personal feeling of failure for him, and your own personal feeling of failure if he turns out to be different from what you thought he would be.

Some of the ways to prevent accepting him for what he is going to be in the future, is to stop making excuses for him, stop justifying the abuse you received from him, and stop making it look like it is your assignment in life to give him what he has never had; Love.

You are not called to make excuses for him, you are not called to justify the abuse you also receive from him, so stop making it look like it is your assignment to make him happy in life.

Set goals for yourself, spiritual, financial, physical, and emotional. If you are single, it is wise to pray that you will not pick a broken man who will turn you to a fixer. Life is already complicated enough as a woman.

They do not accept engagement without being properly courted.

Whoso findeth a wife findeth a good thing, and obtaineth favour of the LORD.
Proverbs 18:22 (KJV)

Pressures do come, and sometimes relationships evolve without following what might be called due process.

It is wise to allow the Lord to lead you at all times, but it is important that you endeavour to allow a man to treat you right, and court you and give you the honour and dignity you deserve, so that things evolve, step by step.

It will be the only testimony you have to hold on to in the future.

They do not become the financier of a man out of desperation.

Within certain cultures a woman might earn more than a man does. If it is a relationship that is not solemnised in marriage, or a courtship, it is wise to understand that a man must show that he truly could be the breadwinner of his house.

Nothing says one cannot court an unemployed person, but it is important that he proves that he deserves your hand. Do not try to keep a man by financing him. He will still leave you if you try to buy him.

They seek spiritual counsel.

*Where no counsel is, the people fall: but in the multitude of
counsellors there is safety.*
Proverbs 11:14 (KJV)

Others have trodden on the road you must tread,
others have been where you must be. You need
mentors to help you make sense of the future. Your
mentors have seen what you are yet to discover, they
have been where you are yet to be.

It is when you surround yourself with good
counselling that your errors are minimized. The
Scriptures cannot be broken, in the multitude of
counsellors you are safe.

Counsellors help you because you have not been
through that way before. They move you from the
ideal life to reality, they help you to know how to
deal with conflict, they minimise your likely stress
or panic when you face battles, because they, by the
grace of God, and with the benefit of experience, are
able to predict how matters will end. Seek pastoral
counselling, your pastor should be your friend.

Draw from the message you hear regularly, do not live by the fountain and fail to drink the water. Also recognise delegated counselling authority established by your church, seek it and practise the advice diligently.

Your life is too precious to depend on 'hair saloon counselling'. Your life is too precious to run it with the gossips from the barber's shop.

They refuse to be secretive and shield off the man's mess.

One of the amazing things about abused women is that some will take it for so long, protecting the man, shielding his falsehood, shielding his lies, and being secretive with him, knowing he is abusive, and possibly sexually promiscuous.

Cases of incest have been known to be properly covered by the mothers of the children being molested.

A godly wise woman does not consider exposure as being wrong because it is in order to bring healing. As a matter of fact it is not exposure, it is making the person vulnerable, so that they will seek help. It is better to lose a person than to cover their mess which will destroy things for generations to come.

How do they expose the mess?

They speak out, they tell the truth but always in love.

Wise women refuse mental, physical, sexual, and financial abuse.

Let no man despise thy youth; but be thou an example of the believers, in word, in conversation, in charity, in spirit, in faith, in purity.
1 Timothy 4:12 (KJV)

In abusive situations the abuser behaves as if it is everyone's fault but him. All his weaknesses he regards as the fault of somebody else. He blames people for his weight, his dad is to blame for being a cheat. The economy is to blame for his overdraft. He lost his job for lateness and it is his parent's fault. He blames God for not growing enough flowers for him to bring to the lady on Valentine's Day.

The wise woman would either stand by him to change or move on, because he would always keep blaming, he might even blame you for picking him. After all, broken people tend to find broken things.

They avoid the trap of comparing the man with their dad, brother or previous boyfriends.

The temptation is there for us to repeat what we have seen before. A girl may not realise how she is likely to marry a man who is a picture of her father, or the most dominant male she ever knew.

It would be dangerous to keep comparing the man to your dad, brother or previous boyfriend because he might either not measure up to them or might be a repeat of what they have done. It is important that you let him be who he is without any pressure.

They do not have unrealistic expectations from the man.

For I say, through the grace given unto me, to every man that is among you, not to think of himself more highly than he ought to think; but to think soberly, according as God hath dealt to every man the measure of faith.
Romans 12:3 (KJV)

A godly wise woman would know that every house is built gradually with wisdom.

Through wisdom is an house builded; and by understanding it is established:
And by knowledge shall the chambers be filled with all precious and pleasant riches.
Proverbs 24:3-4 (KJV)

Unrealistic expectation would mean putting the man under pressure to try to achieve before his time, to try to impress her with what he cannot afford.

Unrealistic expectation would mean making the man live beyond his means, beyond his strength, beyond his ability and in the end bring a disaster upon the relationship.

Wise women avoid rushing to the altar until they court properly.

Why do women rush to the altar quickly? Often times family pressure could make for hasty decisions. The fear of losing the man comes behind that, and thirdly emotional pressure, just the desire to express passion.

Many ladies have also succumbed to peer pressure to do what others have done, or what others want them to do. Waiting for so long is another reason, causing the fear of being left on the shelf, and of being left by the wayside.

Some ladies have panicked because of the fact that their biological cycle is probably indicating that they may be too old to have children.

Some also in certain context and nations have found themselves rushing to the altar, because not too long after the relationship, the man tells them of his immigration status and his need to marry a citizen.

45

Lastly, one wrong reason to go to the altar hastily, is when it is a rebound. That is picking up another relationship, having left one just recently without healing and overcoming the impact of the previous. It is wise to avoid a hasty relationship.

They do not overlook warning signs.

*When wisdom entereth into thine heart, and knowledge is
pleasant unto thy soul;
Discretion shall preserve thee, understanding shall keep
thee:
Proverbs 2:10-11 (KJV)*

My mother's wise saying is that if your eyes bring
out puss when you are a baby it is a bad indication
of how your eyesight might turn out when you are
much older. I do not know if she is right medically,
but so are relationships.

A man who is abusing you physically, who is
dishonest but keeps promising to change. A
"commitment phobic" whose word is not good, who
could never keep to time. His ten o'clock is never
ten, it is actually four. A man whose head is always
in the clouds, talking of the day when he makes his
millions and never lives in the realities of today.

This may be clear warning signs, that there may be
too many issues of the past unresolved which are

now causing a self-esteem problem. Such men refuse to deal with destructive habits, they always have to be in charge and you cannot see enough men around him with whom he has positive relationships.

Such people are afraid to open up, they are not enthusiastic about life, and they are not likely to do for you, as much as you are ready to do for them.

Wise women avoid saying too much too soon.

Wherefore, my beloved brethren, let every man be swift to hear, slow to speak, slow to wrath:
James 1:19 (KJV)

We all have pasts before we meet people with whom we have to have relationships. For some of us it is a past of self-righteousness, for others it is a past of sinfulness. Whatever the past is, we need to know the maturity level of the persons with whom we have to deal, before we over expose the past.

Some are not matured enough to handle the truth about our possible sexual escapades before we got born again, or the people who have gone through our life who left us broken and abused.

We need to know if they are ready to handle what they would hear, and if they are ready to also come clean with us.

Wise women do not pretend to be the perfect Proverbs 31 woman.

Be of the same mind one toward another. Mind not high things, but condescend to men of low estate. Be not wise in your own conceits.
Romans 12:16 (KJV)

A lot of unrealistic men will raise the Proverbs 31 woman as the ideal person they would want. Unknown to them that when you read through the passage, it is more than what a woman can fit into in one day.

The scriptures cannot be broken, the truth in that passage stands. But as we see the several abilities of the Proverbs 31 woman, we see a mirror of what truly we desire to be, but may not be allowed by time, situations, and challenges of modernity.

Wise single women refuse to act like wives ie. washing, cooking, and hosting friends.

Let all things be done decently and in order.
1 Corinthians 14:40 (KJV)

Receive my instruction, and not silver; and knowledge rather
than choice gold.
For wisdom is better than rubies; and all the things that may
be desired are not to be compared to it.
Proverbs 8:10-11 (KJV)

It is important that a courtship be wholesome, that two people who are going out, honour one another, regard one another and respect what each one's values are.

The standard a single woman raises is what a man rises up to. If you start washing when you are not married, if you are busy cooking for him though you are only in courtship, hosting his friends and picking all the dropped *oranges*. Very soon you become a problem solver, when you have no ring on your finger with a commitment that says "I do".

51

Stop chasing after love, stop social actions that suggest such levels of commitment. Refuse to provide any form of sexual favours or actions that may not be wholesome and can make your good to be evil spoken of.

They refuse to display affection before a commitment from the man.

Marriage is honourable in all, and the bed undefiled: but whoremongers and adulterers God will judge.
Hebrews 13:4 (KJV)

If a man is being close and uses statements like "I care for you, you know", "You are really special to me you know". That is not enough to think that there is a relationship going on.

Do not misunderstand a man's hugs and words, if his hugs are becoming one too many it is important to begin to draw the lines. A misunderstanding of men's hugs and words can scare away innocent men.

Men sometimes may use words which they do not process like women will. When a man says "I love you", it may not carry the same weight as it does for a woman. A man can say "I love you" with his body, a woman falls in love spirit, soul and body.

Let the man pursue you, and not you pursue him. Be a responder, do not buy love.

Wise women refuse to break down because of a broken relationship.

Watch ye, stand fast in the faith, quit you like men, be strong.
1 Corinthians 16:13 (KJV)

People come and go, life keeps changing. Many people will pass through our lives. We will reach and contact many.

Relationships are not unlikely, and that is why each stage needs a definition and a right of passage before it goes on to the next. If you are going out with a man, let it be clear and obvious to him and to you that you are still going out.

If it goes beyond that into dating let it be clear and obvious that you are dating each other.

When it is a courtship it should be clear. The engagement needs to be formal so that each level is clearly defined.

Wise women do not live in denial.

They know and they admit when it is over. That is why a wise woman must learn to follow after a man. Events and experience have shown that a woman finds it harder to come out of a relationship than a man. So always be one or two steps behind until you know you have both gone past the point of no return.

They court men who put a woman first.

It is important that you prayerfully consider how a man treats his mother and sister, if he treats them right and gives them due honour as women and as part of his life, it may be an indication that he will treat you right.

It is also important that in his treatment of his family or mother, he puts you first when you are married to him, because the two of you become one flesh, he cannot become one flesh with his mother.

This also means that he refuses disrespect towards you from his family. He makes it clear to them that you are precious to him and he cannot accept any form of disrespect shown you by his relation.

Godly women court men who put them first in purchases, who honour them and spoil them with the little or much that he has.

Godly women are attracted to the man who will never downplay achievement, but rather keep on encouraging them (even when they want to downplay it), until they truly become fulfilled and expressive of what God has done for them.

He remembers that his wife is described as a weaker vessel, and therefore takes up anything that is taxing, painful or burdensome.

Godly women in their wisdom remember that they need a man that will show them honour and treat them always as special.

Wise women do not throw themselves at a man.

Whoso findeth a wife findeth a good thing, and obtaineth favour of the LORD.
Proverbs 18:22 (KJV)

The scriptures say "he who finds a wife finds a good thing". In the game of finders keepers, the man is supposed to be the finder, the woman is the keeper.

If he was the one who sought for you and found you the chances are that he will keep you, and keep honouring you. But if you throw yourself at him you lost your sense of dignity and the joy of being courted and sort after.

Men by nature are hunters, warriors who must seek after what they want. To be bitchy and to pursue a man is to reduce part of the testimony and joy of him giving you due honour

Be dignified, let your husband love you, let him seek after you.

You are a person of dignity, a born again child of the living God. Your name is written in the Book of Life, you are God's princess. You are a woman of honour, a woman of destiny. God has his calling and grace upon your life. Rise to your calling, rise to your level, be a dignified person. Carry yourself according to your destiny.

They stay away from despair when there is a delay.

......weeping may endure for a night, but joy cometh in the morning.
Psalms 30:5b (KJV)

Wisdom must prevail in the management of delays, a wise woman must know that delays are never denials, and because it has not happened does not mean it will not happen.

It is primarily important that you seek the face of God, and establish His call on your life. If we accept it or not we need to know that some of us may have been called to a celibate life, and will only find fulfilment within the scope of our calling.

They know how to pick a man who treats them like a queen.

You live with what you build, you are a mirror of what you choose. Your ability to choose a king to treat you like a queen will determine a lot of things concerning your destiny.

How do you know if a man will treat you right?

A person who will treat you right, must have treated his mother or sisters right.

A man may be the wrong choice if your mother hates him.

A man may be the wrong choice if your pet is scared of him!

The man who thinks that your job is a mere hobby may be wrong. If he is able to provide adequately for the family when you get married that is fine, but if he thinks your job is just a hobby he may not be the right one for you.

If he is racist and sees other races as less than him or above him, he may not be the right person. If he is sexist and chauvinist in his views, be sure he will treat you wrong. If he reminds you of what you are running away from, it is not the best choice to go and live with him.

When a man changes the subject when you talk or pursue your interest, then you know that may not be the right person. You need the man who will treat you like a lady, who would appreciate you like a queen.

Wise women keep believing, trusting and praying to Jesus.

Connecting with the spouse with whom you would live your life must not erode your Christian life, if anything it should enhance it. Whatever reduces your devotion to the Lord may be that which is the beginning of your downfall.

Be wise enough to believe Christ to keep trusting Him and to keep praying to Him.

They do not marry a man who cannot support the family.

But if any provide not for his own, and specially for those of his own house, he hath denied the faith, and is worse than an infidel.
1 Timothy 5:8 (KJV)

The man is called the breadwinner in scriptures, his function is to provide and protect the family. In his calling as the provider, the wife's income must be regarded as supplementary.

A man may be wrong if he is angry that you earn more than he does, some men do not know how to relate to strong women. A man may be wrong if he makes you want to play down your achievement, so as not to hurt his feelings.

The smartest move you would make for yourself will be to call it a day if you are not yet married to him, than to carry on. And if you are married to him, it would be wise to seek how to now build without causing offence to yourself.

Wise women avoid involvement with married men.

Jesus said we must do to others what we expect them to do for us. If you send out a sound expect an echo to come back. Those who sow the wind must be prepared for a harvest of hurricane.

Most times people think that in courting a married man he would leave his wife for them. They do not realise that in the head of a carnal man, there is the desire to have two kinds of women, the one he marries and the one he plays with. Sugar daddies often become sour friends.

The Bible calls any relationship outside of a marriage a sin. You need to define the lines of friendship when you become married and the person you know is married. Avoid the danger of being carried away by the promises he has made to you.

He may be using you as an escape valve from the pressures at home, he may be using you as an escape valve for the times when he is denied conjugal love and he is likely to warm up to his wife when the heat is over. You become the wounded lady who was used, abused and dumped by the roadside.

They are wise to say no in courtship to things they do not want in marriage.

Open rebuke is better than secret love.
Proverbs 27:5 (KJV)

It is interesting how many women will push the responsibility of discovering what a man is likely to be in marriage to God. They make statements like "If God had shown me that he was this wicked, I would not have gone into it". Whereas on the other hand there may have been clear indications that a woman's ship was heading for a disastrous headlong collision with an iceberg, but she refused to do the right things.

How do you know? There are many reasons or ways to know when a relationship is not right. A relationship is not right:

If the man keeps beating you when he downplays your success.

He constantly puts you down.

He has no plans for your own needs.

He treats you as if you are the same level or lesser than his car. He gives more attention to the car, shines it, polishes it, takes care of it, spends extra money on it, but raises his voice every time you talk to him.

He acts like he is emotionless, he gives sarcastic nicknames to you. He is very critical of your appearance, he does not like your friends, your family, your home and he makes fun of your personality and performance. He simply does not want to understand that you are precious and should be treated that way.

He also does not understand the concept of forgiveness, so when you are wrong he never lets go, and when he is wrong he lacks the emotion to back his remorse. He blames everyone but himself for what life has delivered to him, and you feel like he has taken over your life.

It is time to say no to beating, no to any form of abuse, and no to a man who will take you to a marriage that will only end in disaster.

They do not discuss or compare old and new boyfriends.

Therefore if any man be in Christ, he is a new creature: old things are passed away; behold, all things are become new.
2 Corinthians 5:17 (KJV)

A man may be able to stand many things and take a lot of abuse, but he certainly will not be able to take your attitude of comparing him with other men.

Your spouse may have an innate hatred for any man you respect or honour, because while on one hand he does not get all the attention, affection, love and care, he thinks he deserves from you, yet you come home and speak so highly of other men in your life.

They are wise enough to avoid interrogating the man about previous girlfriends.

Therefore if any man be in Christ, he is a new creature: old things are passed away; behold, all things are become new.
2 Corinthians 5:17 (KJV)

By the time many of us came in contact with the gospel we already have certain experiences that are not honouring to the Lord. After salvation, it is important to remember the change the finished work of Jesus has brought.

If you keep bringing old girlfriends up to your spouse or fiancé your actions suggest jealousy. It may reveal the insecurities you have, and a lack of self-esteem. Such actions may ruin the future because things keep coming up from your past and his.

If you must deal with matters from the past in his or your life, let such information come up at such times when it is appropriate for healing and progress.

They are wise enough not to allow their insecurities to destroy their future.

The things we have gone through in life tend to shape us, and if you have been disappointed by the opposite sex it raises the chances of insecurities.

Many relationships have been quashed; many people who would have been great winning partners have themselves frustrated what started well, because they allowed the insecurities born out of their experience to destroy a good thing coming together for them.

The wise single woman does not confuse friendship with courtship.

Some men are fond of using words like "you mean a lot to me", "I hold you in high esteem", "you are my precious sister", "agape love", and "I have the God kind of love for you".

All this to a lady may mean he simply does not know how to put his words together and say "I love you", and therefore every statement he makes is being read into, misunderstood, as if a courtship has started.

He is probably speaking in a way that is not clear and she is carrying along in her own mind with the thought "we are already in courtship". And whereas there may have been no relationship whatsoever.

They do not replace a man's mother.

It is very frustrating for a man to be treated as if he is still a child. Many women who have probably lived with a child for long, especially single parents, do not know how to transition from talking to their little boys to now talking to the man who is their husband.

You may be treating him like a child when you help him too much and make him look like he is hopeless, making statements that suggest he is forgetful like a boy. "Do not forget to lock the door", "remember to put the rubbish bag outside". When you tell a man off like a child you remind him of his mother and you are acting in her place.

Some ladies forget that this is their husband, and make statements like "how many times do I have to remind you to pay the bill". The woman who has a strong personality married to a phlegmatic man will find herself taking over certain duties believing that he will not do it right.

They become over-bearing wives who make all the decisions, believing that their husbands are incapable. They yell out direction and correction, and they say it is in their nature to do it, but they forget the boundaries which should be out there.

A woman has to understand that the nurturing instinct of a woman in her is what may be at play. She did not mean evil, but it would turn the man against you if you do not know when or where it stops.

It will bring you in conflict with the calling of a warrior that is on your husband's life or your fiancé's life. Some men will allow it because of childhood inadequacies, but the consequence is a paralysis of his person and an eventual immaturity.

He will not be able to love you in a matured way in later years.

Wise women avoid seeking expensive gifts as a sign of love and commitment.

The priority in any relationship must be the heart and not the purse. Whether he takes you to a fast food restaurant or an expensive restaurant, it is not the kind of gifts with which he showers you, but the kind of heart from which it comes and the constancy of it.

The regularity of it matters a lot, but not to begin to measure how expensive it is.

Whatever a man does should be in proportion to the love he shows you and his commitment to you.

They are wise enough not to throw away a diamond that looks rough.

And when the children of Israel saw it, they said one to another, It is manna: for they wist not what it was. And Moses said unto them, This is the bread which the LORD hath given you to eat.
Exodus 16:15 (KJV)

In spite of the adage not to judge something by its wrapping, today's marketing and packaging has shaped and influenced our thinking. We buy things purely because of the way they are presented to us, and what we are told they can do, even when we are not sure.

We bring the same philosophy and attitude into our relationships and things that will shape our destiny. We marry men we may not be totally proud of sometimes because all we were looking at was how handsome they are.

While on another hand we may meet a man who is a diamond in the rough, by the way, diamonds never look glittery. A diamond was once coal that went through a lot of heat and became a stone in the rough, was chippened until the beauty came out.

If you must marry it is important to like what you see, but firstly do not be carried away by outward looks. Do not be carried away by your critical opinion. When the children of Israel saw the food that was dropped from heaven their first response was "manna" which really means, "what is this?"

If you keep focusing at a man's point of social acceptance and social measure, you might miss a diamond. If you keep looking at his present educational, physical, and financial status you might miss a diamond.

A girl dumped Billy Graham in college because she thought college boys were not serious.

Wise women avoid being terminators or destroyers of the warrior spirit in their man.

Male chauvinism is not right, yet a man by nature is made by God to be a warrior. A wise woman will let the man be the pursuant.

She would let him suggest and run around for special occasions.

A wise woman would stop worrying about if she is the one who is right or wrong for this person.

At such times when a person is worried they try to please the man they are romantically attached to and in the end make mistakes. Do not help him to fulfil the romantic blank, let him pursue, let him show that he deserves your hand. Do not kill the warrior spirit in him; do not deny him the ability to use his potential either.

Many women do this by allowing issues that were

unresolved from their past to encroach on their future. Do not criticise present lovers with things from previous relationships, and if you are married do not bring issues up late at night.

There is a time to reach a man, there is a time to address issues. Do not call it a short discussion and then keep going on and on, that switches a man off. Your spouse likes to feel he is independent, so there is a time to be quiet.

Do not attack him because he does not notice details like you do, men have a different way of processing information. Give the man a lot of positive feedback if he opens his vulnerabilities to you. Do not do more for him than he does for you though, it is important that marriage be a point of mutual exchange and love.

Ruth walked in the friendship that is the foundation for a healthy relationship.

You cannot live your life in isolation, that is why God surrounds you with people. You must be able to have friends, who will validate you, encourage you, and help you to be a winner.

Healthy relationships are necessary to be a healthy person. Your social contacts are an indication of how you have chosen to make your life work.

Ruth had Naomi, who in spite of storms was still standing; she became a good example to Ruth that troubles should not stop you, because troubles do not last forever.

Ruth had Boaz, a man who challenged her to know that there are still people of integrity, credibility and honesty.

Godly women stand with people through their hard times.

And they lifted up their voice, and wept again: and Orpah
kissed her mother in law; but Ruth clave unto her.
Ruth 1:14 (KJV)

Two women determined their destinies by their choice when the person they had to relate to came face to face with hard times. Orpah kissed her mother-in-law and walked into oblivion. Ruth risked her future but walked into a great destiny and fame.

Godly women do not become neutral when their friends are in trouble. They do not run away from involvement when the people they love are in trouble, or shy away from responsibility when people they love are in trouble.

Your ability to become a bridge to people's troubled water marks you out for distinction.

Godly women are people of loyalty and commitment.

*And Ruth said, Intreat me not to leave thee, or to return
from following after thee: for whither thou goest, I will go;
and where thou lodgest, I will lodge: thy people shall be my
people, and thy God my God:*
*Where thou diest, will I die, and there will I be buried: the
LORD do so to me, and more also, if ought but death part
thee and me.*
Ruth 1:16-17 (KJV)

Loyalty and commitment are higher than mere
involvement. Godly women choose their
relationships and once they find it they show loyalty
and total commitment.

Ruth was willing to walk away from what she knew
into what she had never experienced, because of her
loyalty to the mentor she found.

The faithful man is said to abound in blessing,
disloyalty will result in betrayal and when you
betray others you might reap the fruit of the seed
you have sown.

A godly woman has an unflinching commitment to the Lord.

And Ruth said, Intreat me not to leave thee, or to return from following after thee: for whither thou goest, I will go; and where thou lodgest, I will lodge: thy people shall be my people, and thy God my God:
Ruth 1:17 (KJV)

What marks you out as being committed is your relationship with the Lord. What marks you out as being usable for the Lord is your commitment to the Lord.

People who are committed to the Lord become amiable; they become accessible to God. God is not looking for a majority but those who are committed to His calling and purpose for their lives.

A wise woman builds relationships that are based on values not valuables.

Relationships built on valuables do not last, they vanish when the things are gone. Relationships built on valuables have no strength; it is like building your house upon the sand. It will not be able to stand the storms and the hassles; the elements will tear it apart.

When you put value to your relationships, you make marriage work. Putting values to your relationships means improving relationships with people. Set goals for your future relationships with people, plan for your children, develop common views with your spouse.

Godly women are marked by their ability to keep promises.

Lie not one to another, seeing that ye have put off the old man with his deeds;
Colossians 3:9 (KJV)

The true worth of a person is the ability to keep promises. God is only as good as His Word. A godly woman will be measured not by her externals, but by her ability to stay true to the promises she has made.

Godly women allow the Lord to lead them to His favour.

And Naomi had a kinsman of her husband's, a mighty man of wealth, of the family of Elimelech; and his name was Boaz.
Ruth 2:1 (KJV)

Every breakthrough you set up yourself will come back and hurt you, anything of your own imagination can work against you. A favour obtained by God cannot be stolen, destroyed or aborted. Godly women know that if it is the Lord who has set you up for blessing, no man can frustrate your destiny.

God has promised to put a difference between those who know Him and those who do not.

Thou shalt arise, and have mercy upon Zion: for the time to favour her, yea, the set time, is come.
For thy servants take pleasure in her stones, and favour the dust thereof.
Psalms 102:13-14 (KJV)

They relate to men who honour God and them with their substance.

And Boaz said unto her, At mealtime come thou hither, and eat of the bread, and dip thy morsel in the vinegar. And she sat beside the reapers: and he reached her parched corn, and she did eat, and was sufficed, and left.
And when she was risen up to glean, Boaz commanded his young men, saying, Let her glean even among the sheaves, and reproach her not:
And let fall also some of the handfuls of purpose for her, and leave them, that she may glean them, and rebuke her not.
Ruth 2:14-16 (KJV)

You will provoke what is essentially in a man, you raise him to the standard you have lifted for yourself. A spouse who withholds his substance from worshipping God with it, hinders the blessing of the Lord upon the family.

A godly woman stands by her husband and challenges him to hourly obedience, so that the blessing of the Lord might rest upon their home.

Godly women know how to find a man of extra care and compassion.

And Boaz said unto her, At mealtime come thou hither, and eat of the bread, and dip thy morsel in the vinegar. And she sat beside the reapers: and he reached her parched corn, and she did eat, and was sufficed, and left.
And when she was risen up to glean, Boaz commanded his young men, saying, Let her glean even among the sheaves, and reproach her not: And let fall also some of the handfuls of purpose for her, and leave them, that she may glean them, and rebuke her not.   Ruth 2:14-16 (KJV)

Women have a greater discernment than men, they can smell trouble from a long distance. A man may walk into the zone of temptation much easier than the woman would have done. It is wise for a woman to direct that ability in her choice of the man with whom she will share her future.

To know that she must look for care and compassion above the ethereal and physical comfort he may promise.

A godly woman truly knows a good man when she sees one.

They are committed to a vow and covenant of oneness.

Where thou diest, will I die, and there will I be buried: the LORD do so to me, and more also, if ought but death part thee and me.
Ruth 1:17 (KJV)

The scriptures say two shall become one flesh, the process of one fleshness is a lifetime experience. While positionally it happens at the exchange of vows, it takes a deliberate act of commitment to the vow made for it to become experiential.

The place of unity is the place of power. A godly wise woman seeks for people with whom she can truly walk in unity and network with them.

Behold, how good and how pleasant it is for brethren to dwell together in unity!
It is like the precious ointment upon the head, that ran down upon the beard, even Aaron's beard: that went down to the skirts of his garments;
As the dew of Hermon, and as the dew that descended upon the mountains of Zion: for there the LORD commanded the blessing, even life for evermore.
Psalms 133:1-3 (KJV)

Godly women are attracted to godly men as carnal women are attracted to carnal men.

And, behold, Boaz came from Bethlehem, and said unto the reapers, The LORD be with you. And they answered him, The LORD bless thee.
Then said Boaz unto his servant that was set over the reapers, Whose damsel is this?
And the servant that was set over the reapers answered and said, It is the Moabitish damsel that came back with Naomi out of the country of Moab:
And she said, I pray you, let me glean and gather after the reapers among the sheaves: so she came, and hath continued even from the morning until now, that she tarried a little in the house.
Then said Boaz unto Ruth, Hearest thou not, my daughter? Go not to glean in another field, neither go from hence, but abide here fast by my maidens:
Ruth 2:4-8 (KJV)

Spirit talks to spirit, flesh to flesh, what you are is what you attract. If you raise your standard and pursue God and His will, you have automatically raised the quality of what will come towards you. The irony of it is that people tend to complain when

they have attracted the wrong, but fail to realise that
they have by all signs and actions indicated what
they might get.

Godly women are marked by their diligence.

And she said, I pray you, let me glean and gather after the reapers among the sheaves: so she came, and hath continued even from the morning until now, that she tarried a little in the house.
Ruth 2:7 (KJV)

So she gleaned in the field until even, and beat out that she had gleaned: and it was about an ephah of barley.
Ruth 2:17 (KJV)

Ruth stood out in the vineyard of Boaz, not for being troublesome, but for diligence. Diligence is the quality that would lift you to the level of success.

God is a worker and those who know Him would express His nature and life. Diligence qualifies you for leadership, diligence qualifies your service to God.

Not slothful in business; fervent in spirit; serving the Lord;
Romans 12:11 (KJV)

Diligence multiplies God's grace in you.

And beside this, giving all diligence, add to your faith virtue;
and to virtue knowledge;
2 Peter 1:5 (KJV)

Diligence exposes the gift and calling of God on your life.

Wherefore the rather, brethren, give diligence to make your
calling and election sure: for if ye do these things, ye shall
never fall:
2 Peter 1:10 (KJV)

Some people dream of accomplishments, godly women stay up to make it happen.

Diligence protects your heart from contamination.

Keep thy heart with all diligence; for out of it are the issues
of life.
Proverbs 4:23 (KJV)

Diligence is your doorway to prosperity.

The soul of the sluggard desireth, and hath nothing: but the
soul of the diligent shall be made fat.
Proverbs 13:4 (KJV)

The only thing that gets results is work not wish.

Godly women attract outstanding compassion.

And she said, I pray you, let me glean and gather after the reapers among the sheaves: so she came, and hath continued even from the morning until now, that she tarried a little in the house.
Ruth 2:7 (KJV)

So she gleaned in the field until even, and beat out that she had gleaned: and it was about an ephah of barley.
Ruth 2:17 (KJV)

In a farm where many labourers may have been turned away. Ruth stood out for her godliness and she attracted favour and compassion. Godly women move away from the grief of the past.

With three deaths in the family Ruth probably had every emotional right to walk in grief and live a broken life. In the same vein she recognised that the grief you walk in may ruin the joy you should know.

If you are unable to let go of grief, you implode and self-destruct.

Godly women draw strength from the Lord to be able to mourn at the time of mourning, but rejoice when it should follow.

Many women tend to hold on to dead issues, dead relationships and dead situations. The mark of godliness will be your ability to let go of those dead issues and receive the healing of the Lord.

Godly women know that their diligence opens greater doors.

Then said Boaz unto Ruth, Hearest thou not, my daughter?
Go not to glean in another field, neither go from hence, but
abide here fast by my maidens:
Ruth 2:8 (KJV)

It is foolish to expect a reward in excess of your contribution, your contribution determines your reward.

The problem you solve determines the blessing you receive; the problem you solve determines the promise fulfilled in your life. Your access to prosperity is by diligence. It raises your level of achievement.

Diligence is your passport to being in front.

That is why Solomon concluded that:

The hand of the diligent shall bear rule: but the slothful shall
be under tribute.
Proverbs 12:24 (KJV)

Godly women have an eye for true protectors.

Then said Boaz unto Ruth, Hearest thou not, my daughter?
Go not to glean in another field, neither go from hence, but
abide here fast by my maidens:
Ruth 2:8 (KJV)

A human protector is a person to stand with you.

A person to take the heat.

It is the person who answers when the enemy knocks at the door.

It is not enough to choose a spouse, it is important to choose the person who truly will stand and fight the good fight of faith until you win or win together.

Godly women go the extra mile in their humility.

Then she fell on her face, and bowed herself to the ground, and said unto him, Why have I found grace in thine eyes, that thou shouldest take knowledge of me, seeing I am a stranger?
Ruth 2:10 (KJV)

Ruth's humility and submission to Boaz opened the door of grace and caused her to find favour everywhere she turned.

Humility will make people overlook weaknesses, and suspicions. Humility will cause a stranger to be treated as the host of the house.

God sees the proud afar off but draws near to those that are of a humble heart. The woman who fears the Lord, she shall be praised.

Their sacrifice is matched by their breakthrough.

And Boaz answered and said unto her, It hath fully been shewed me, all that thou hast done unto thy mother in law since the death of thine husband: and how thou hast left thy father and thy mother, and the land of thy nativity, and art come unto a people which thou knewest not heretofore.
Ruth 2:11 (KJV)

What you are willing to walk away from determines what you bump into, what you lay on the altar will provoke what resurrects for you.

The seed that goes out of your hands already preconditions the harvest that comes to your life.

Ruth was willing to leave behind her father and mother, she was willing to walk away from the land of her nativity in order to experience the destiny God had for her.

Your unwillingness to move away from your familiar grounds may make you not to discover new territories. Until your ship sails out you may not find new shores.

Such sailing out may be a sacrifice, but the fruit that will follow will be the breakthrough.

They are investors who take care and save for the future.

And Boaz said unto her, At mealtime come thou hither, and eat of the bread, and dip thy morsel in the vinegar. And she sat beside the reapers: and he reached her parched corn, and she did eat, and was sufficed, and left.
Ruth 2:14 (KJV)

Go to the ant, thou sluggard; consider her ways, and be wise:
Proverbs 6:6 (KJV)

She considereth a field, and buyeth it: with the fruit of her hands she planteth a vineyard.
Proverbs 31:16 (KJV)

- Know that good years must pay for bad years.
- Never have a zero month.
- God gives seed so it can become trees.
- Creating wealth is for a purpose.
- So that you can be a lender and not a borrower
- God who saved you from sin has given you the power to get wealth.
- The power of leaving an inheritance
- To start and perpetuate generational blessing.
- Providing a future of comfort.

Godly women choose husbands who will be truly a sheltering wing.

Boaz provided the security Ruth needed, he provided the atmosphere for the joy she was to walk in.

She withstood the hard times with her faith and she received the blessing of trusting in the God who provides.

There was such a massive age gap that he called her his daughter, yet Boaz treated her as a woman of virtue.

And now, my daughter, fear not; I will do to thee all that thou requirest: for all the city of my people doth know that thou art a virtuous woman.
Ruth 3:11 (KJV)

Godly women make their purpose in life to be their greatest pursuit.

And the servant that was set over the reapers answered and said, It is the Moabitish damsel that came back with Naomi out of the country of Moab:
And she said, I pray you, let me glean and gather after the reapers among the sheaves: so she came, and hath continued even from the morning until now, that she tarried a little in the house.
Ruth 2:6-7 (KJV)

What you call a thing sometimes determines how it turns out. When Ruth's parent gave her the name which means "friendship", they probably did not realise how her destiny was to be shaped by a name so simple.

The willingness to make Naomi a friend in adversity was a revelation of the destiny and purpose which she carried.

The Moabitess damsel who now comes to find a husband in a distant country, and through that becomes the woman through whom David comes to the world is subsequently mentioned in the lineage of Jesus.

Godly women seek and pursue their purpose, they know their future is only fulfilled not in the abundance of activity, but in the knowledge and pursuit of their purpose on earth.

Godly women are willing to set a high standard.

And when she was risen up to glean, Boaz commanded his
young men, saying, Let her glean even among the sheaves,
and reproach her not:
Ruth 2:15 (KJV)

Men who sometimes will pursue a woman without
virtue will yet in private admit that they prefer the
one of virtue to live with. Ruth raised a standard so
high.

It is the standard you raise that the man you meet
and marry will have to rise up to. Ruth was above
reproach, Ruth defined her standard, she was not to
be pushed around by the young men in town.

Adversity may have exposed you to temptation, but
it would not lead you into it. It is your choice to
raise a standard and refuse to compromise in spite of
what you go through.

Godly women recognise that what they look like should bring respect and recognition.

People do not judge the content first; they start with the packaging. Vulgarity will not bring respect, neither would it command recognition.

Nonetheless the scripture is not against dressing to be attractive; it is only against dressing to get attention.

They recognise and pursue where grace and mercy has been ordained for them.

It is important to go where you are honoured. It is important to be where you are celebrated, not tolerated. Mercy and grace has been ordained for you, locate it and enjoy it. Not in any other field, but where you have been destined to receive your harvest.

The mark of a godly woman is the ability to discern where favour exists and to pursue diligently until she receives.

They know that someone is observing their quality of work, and level of diligence.

So she kept fast by the maidens of Boaz to glean unto the end of barley harvest and of wheat harvest; and dwelt with her mother in law.
Ruth 2:23 (KJV)

Someone is always observing your level of diligence, they may not comment now, but your work will speak for you. A godly woman is marked by her commitment to her God-ordained vision.

She is known by the quality and impact she makes, by the service she provides.

We see her in Proverbs 31:

Who can find a virtuous woman? for her price is far above rubies. The heart of her husband doth safely trust in her, so that he shall have no need of spoil.
She will do him good and not evil all the days of her life.
She seeketh wool, and flax, and worketh willingly with her hands.
She is like the merchants' ships; she bringeth her food from afar.

She riseth also while it is yet night, and giveth meat to her household, and a portion to her maidens.
She considereth a field, and buyeth it: with the fruit of her hands she planteth a vineyard.
She girdeth her loins with strength, and strengtheneth her arms. She perceiveth that her merchandise is good: her candle goeth not out by night.
She layeth her hands to the spindle, and her hands hold the distaff. She stretcheth out her hand to the poor; yea, she reacheth forth her hands to the needy.
She is not afraid of the snow for her household: for all her household are clothed with scarlet.
She maketh herself coverings of tapestry; her clothing is silk and purple. Her husband is known in the gates, when he sitteth among the elders of the land.
She maketh fine linen, and selleth it; and delivereth girdles unto the merchant. Strength and honour are her clothing; and she shall rejoice in time to come.
She openeth her mouth with wisdom; and in her tongue is the law of kindness. She looketh well to the ways of her household, and eateth not the bread of idleness. Her children rise up, and call her blessed; her husband also, and he praiseth her.
Many daughters have done virtuously, but thou excellest them all. Favour is deceitful, and beauty is vain: but a woman that feareth the LORD, she shall be praised.
Give her of the fruit of her hands; and let her own works praise her in the gates.
Proverbs 31:10-31 (KJV)

Godly women know that there is a time of winnowing when God separates the good from the bad, the grain from the chaff.

And now is not Boaz of our kindred, with whose maidens thou wast? Behold, he winnoweth barley to night in the threshingfloor.
Ruth 3:2 (KJV)

The knowledge of separation provokes a two dimensional understanding. Firstly it helps us to understand that good will outlast the bad. There is a time not to respond to the evil that men do to us, but to leave the vengeance to God because He is able to separate the good from the bad.

It also drives home the fact that there is a harvest of souls coming when God will take those who are His, and therefore it provokes in the godly woman a desire to serve the Lord and to wait for His appearance.

Godly women know that to be desired you have to make yourself desirable - wash, anoint, dress.

Wash thyself therefore, and anoint thee, and put thy raiment upon thee, and get thee down to the floor: but make not thyself known unto the man, until he shall have done eating and drinking.
Ruth 3:3 (KJV)

The subject of Christian dressing has in the past divided the Body of Christ, and those who bore the brunt of it were most times the women.

While men will dress and look sharp, they make demands that the woman's dress be long and shabby, covering every part as if seeing a woman would cause you to be tempted immediately.

Often times scriptures were misused and the most popular for such men was Deuteronomy 22:5

The woman shall not wear that which pertaineth unto a man, neither shall a man put on a woman's garment: for all that do so are abomination unto the LORD thy God.
Deuteronomy 22:5 (KJV)

Which itself can not be properly interpreted unless one literally interprets all the verses previous and after in the same chapter. Ruth on the other hand was told by her mother-in-law to prepare herself to be a testimony.

If you are married certain qualities attracted your spouse, they need not leave because you are now married, if anything, they need to be enhanced.

Certain qualities attract a man to a single lady, and because men are often influenced and impressed by what they see, the lady needs to be spiritual but also needs to understand the importance of physical attractiveness.

Beauty is a matter of interpretation, just a little working on oneself can change the total outlook of life.

Godly women recognise that the outward is often a mirror of the soul.

Wash thyself therefore, and anoint thee, and put thy raiment upon thee, and get thee down to the floor: but make not thyself known unto the man, until he shall have done eating and drinking.
Ruth 3:3 (KJV)

It is interesting to note that a woman's hair is the first picture of who she is. How you take care of your physical person. How faithful and diligent you are to ensure that the quality of the person people see is always clean and healthy, may be a mirror of a healthy soul that has found its strength in knowing God.

A godly woman is willing to sacrifice feminine pride for generational blessing.

Wash thyself therefore, and anoint thee, and put thy raiment upon thee, and get thee down to the floor: but make not thyself known unto the man, until he shall have done eating and drinking.
Ruth 3:3 (KJV)

The Bible order for meeting the man of your life is that the man should find you, the discovery should come from him. Men should be the hunters while the woman should be the responder.

A man is a warrior, and if he is, he should go out and look for the lady he should marry. In Ruth's case, because of her peculiar situation and on this occasion because it was to become a testimony, her ability and willingness to die to her feminine pride was what provoked and produced generational blessing.

A godly woman knows and moves with the man who will not isolate her.

And when Boaz had eaten and drunk, and his heart was merry, he went to lie down at the end of the heap of corn: and she came softly, and uncovered his feet, and laid her down.
Ruth 3:7 (KJV)

Godly women will wisely pick the man they will share their future with. If you pick a man who himself is fighting with his self-esteem, he is likely to isolate you and prevent you from meeting those who will challenge you and help you to be a better person.

The qualities to look for in the man you will share your future with, among others should be vision and honour.

A godly woman knows the necessity for courting an emotionally healthy person.

And now, my daughter, fear not; I will do to thee all that thou requirest: for all the city of my people doth know that thou art a virtuous woman.
And now it is true that I am thy near kinsman: howbeit there is a kinsman nearer than I.
Tarry this night, and it shall be in the morning, that if he will perform unto thee the part of a kinsman, well; let him do the kinsman's part: but if he will not do the part of a kinsman to thee, then will I do the part of a kinsman to thee, as the LORD liveth: lie down until the morning.
Ruth 3:11-13 (KJV)

Boaz did not take advantage of a single woman who was in the vicinity of where he was. He did not embarrass, molest or abuse Ruth.

He was willing to let a relative who had the first choice make up his mind.

Godly and wise women make decisions that honour God in their choice of the person they will live with. Men also could be possessive or walk in pathological jealousy.

Boaz was willing to let God's will be done and let the other relation express his desire. A godly woman would not need to help God, she knows that if it is of the Lord, He will perfect what He begins.

To choose a healthy person you must yourself be one. It is important to deal with inner issues that are still disturbing, so that they do not mislead you to take the wrong steps.

She knows that there is a positive pay day for maintaining a no compromise stand.

And now, my daughter, fear not; I will do to thee all that thou requirest: for all the city of my people doth know that thou art a virtuous woman.
Ruth 3:11 (KJV)

The testimony of her virtue was known to everyone in town, people may not say it out, but they know what you stand for. Your actions are louder than your voice.

If you stand for nothing you will fall for anything. You are not at a loss if you choose to live a virtuous life and walk in purity. A single girl must not have to compromise because she wants a man to be her husband. If he dishonours you in courtship, he will defile your bed of marriage.

She knows that the will of God is to be preferred to looks, or status.

Favour is deceitful, and beauty is vain: but a woman that feareth the LORD, she shall be praised.
Proverbs 31:30 (KJV)

The words of Boaz are very revealing, there must have been an age gap between him and Ruth. It was not his wealth that attracted her, neither was it his looks, but her mentor endorsed him. He was a godly man, he had a testimony in town, he was diligent.

It is important that as godly women who are single and trusting God, not to put all your trust in what people look like or what status they command.

It is important to see how they have made other people's life productive, how they have influenced the people around them. It is important to recognise their destiny and their pursuit of it. That is the best thing to influence the choice of a godly woman.

Recognise that your Isaac blessing may be preceded by an Ishmael.

*And now it is true that I am thy near kinsman: howbeit there
is a kinsman nearer than I.*
Ruth 3:12 (KJV)

The days of waiting on the Lord in praying, fasting
and seeking His face could expose you in the spirit
realm to a likely proposal that may not be ordained
of God.

Ishmael preceded Isaac, sometimes what you did not
bargain for may come first. It may look all inch like
what you wanted, but there will always be an
indication by the Holy Spirit that this is not it. If
what you finally are supposed to settle for does not
have immediate manifestation like what you first
found, it is important to listen to the Holy Spirit who
Himself knows the heart of all men, and can lead
you perfectly. Paul said:

*For as many as are led by the Spirit of God, they are the
sons of God.*
Romans 8:14 (KJV)

Godly women know and relate to men who will not violate them sexually.

And she lay at his feet until the morning: and she rose up before one could know another. And he said, Let it not be known that a woman came into the floor.
Ruth 3:14 (KJV)

Ruth was attracted to Boaz and vice versa. Productive men tend to pick productive women. If you always attract men who abuse you or are violent towards you, could you have been sending out the wrong message?

A godly woman will go before the Lord and ask for His healing and deliverance, so that next time a man knocks, it is the one who will treat you like a lady and give you the ultimate honour.

Godly women are concerned that their relationship only bring honour.

And he took ten men of the elders of the city, and said, Sit ye down here. And they sat down.
Ruth 4:2 (KJV)

And Boaz said unto the elders, and unto all the people, Ye are witnesses this day, that I have bought all that was Elimelech's, and all that was Chilion's and Mahlon's, of the hand of Naomi.
Ruth 4:9 (KJV)

Rise to your calling, rise to your level, be a dignified person. Carry yourself according to your destiny.

If it is taking long to get into such relationship then remember that it is worth the wait.

A five-course meal is worth the wait than a hasty snack.

Godly women are only concerned that their actions bring generational blessing not a curse.

Today's actions are tomorrow's harvest. What you do today becomes your children's harvest in the future. Many are under the burden of a generational curse which is a by-product of what their grandfathers did.

God said He visits the sin of the fathers on their children to the third and fourth generation. Actions provoke generational curses and they also instigate generational blessings.

The blessing of the Lord can make you become a testimony like Rachel and Leah who became the point of reference in the house of Israel.

Your actions will provoke generational blessing as you serve the Lord; your actions provoke generational blessing as you walk in hourly obedience; they provoke generational blessing as you train your children in the way which they should go, so they do not depart from the counsel of the Lord.

She knows that her limitation is a chance for God to prove Himself.

*And let thy house be like the house of Pharez, whom Tamar
bare unto Judah, of the seed which the LORD shall give thee
of this young woman.*
Ruth 4:12 (KJV)

Your weakness can become the entry point for the
enemy, or the point from which God proves Himself
in your life. Your friends who turn against you may
want to use your point of weakness, but it is also the
point from which you can solicit God's help.

A godly wise woman will turn over her weaknesses
to God and not seek to justify it.

*And he said unto me, My grace is sufficient for thee: for my
strength is made perfect in weakness. Most gladly therefore
will I rather glory in my infirmities, that the power of Christ
may rest upon me.*
*Therefore I take pleasure in infirmities, in reproaches, in
necessities, in persecutions, in distresses for Christ's sake: for
when I am weak, then am I strong.*
2 Corinthians 12:9-10 (KJV)

The quality of Ruth's life outshone that of seven sons.

And let thy house be like the house of Pharez, whom Tamar bare unto Judah, of the seed which the LORD shall give thee of this young woman.
Ruth 4:12 (KJV)

A married woman's response to her mother-in-law says a lot about her. Some mother-in-laws want to control their sons. The ability to have found a mentor in her mother-in-law must have been a testimony to the person Ruth was.

In the Hebrew culture sons are the pride of mothers; their strength in old age; sons are the testimony of mothers. Ruth was said to have outshined seven sons by the actions of her life.

When you are faced with the challenge of in-laws, remember it is not the best scenario to be living together with them. Do not borrow from them, it is wise not to live next door to your in-laws.

Make efforts to sever every umbilical cord that ties

you unncessarily to your parents. Do not
transfer the expectations you have had from your
dad to your husband. If your parents or his are
immature, it is important that you both take steps to
safeguard your marriage.

No matter how positive, avoid any over involvement
of your in-laws, and where one-parent still wants to
be the centre of attraction, it is wise to learn to
break that cord, and both of you should leave home
and cleave to one another.

Godly women bring new joy to dead wombs, old hands and dead situations.

And Naomi took the child, and laid it in her bosom, and became nurse unto it.
Ruth 4:16 (KJV)

Naomi was a type and a shadow of the past; the old guard. She was a picture of a dead situation, something which no longer functions. Ruth was her connection to the future, Ruth was her connection to joy.

Godly women in the wisdom and grace that is upon them, have learnt to bring dead wombs alive.

They have learnt to bring laughter where there was none. Healing where there was hurt; hope to the hopeless.

It is not enough that you have found health and joy for your personal life. It is important that your Christian life now reflects the grace of God, the hand of God, and the new thing He is doing in you and through you.

Godly women know that God can take you from where nothing is working for you - age, widowhood, no child, foreigner - to become first class.

It is not over with God until it is over, just because it is dark today does not mean that light would not shine. Every time the sky is dark, the light shines elsewhere, the sun never disappears it is just covered momentarily.

Age need not be a barrier; widowhood must not stop you. Because there is no child today does not mean there will never be. A person in a foreign land can still prosper, ask Joseph, Daniel, or Nehemiah.

So from the back of the crowd, the godly woman who knows her connection is not compromised, but God can move her to the front, from the last to first class.

It will take an understanding of the principles of mentoring and the willingness to follow the counsel of the person who has been ahead.

The law of location says, "there is a chosen location for your assignment and blessing".

*Those that be planted in the house of the LORD shall
flourish in the courts of our God.
Psalms 92:13 (KJV)*

Godly women are devoted to family.

And she said, Behold, thy sister in law is gone back unto her people, and unto her gods: return thou after thy sister in law.
And Ruth said, Intreat me not to leave thee, or to return from following after thee: for whither thou goest, I will go; and where thou lodgest, I will lodge: thy people shall be my people, and thy God my God:
Where thou diest, will I die, and there will I be buried: the LORD do so to me, and more also, if ought but death part thee and me.
When she saw that she was stedfastly minded to go with her, then she left speaking unto her.
Ruth 1:15-18 (KJV)

The heart of a godly woman is the upkeep of her family. It is the raising of her home. The first devotion of a godly woman is to raise a home where Jesus is Lord and God is glorified.

It is important to prioritise for your family, and to know that you have not succeeded until you have at home with your spouse and children. Charity must begin at home.

She takes delight in her assignment.

And Ruth the Moabitess said unto Naomi, Let me now go to the field, and glean ears of corn after him in whose sight I shall find grace. And she said unto her, Go, my daughter.
Ruth 2:2 (KJV)

The order of scripture is that man is the provider for his family. Adam and Eve fell when she replaced him in that role and provided the apple for the family.

The modern man is confronted with the fact that he has to work, and if it becomes necessary a woman must work to supplement her husband's income. The argument may be out there that suppose she earns more than him.

The role must not change because of the pay packet, the man is called the breadwinner. Nonetheless, a godly woman takes delight in the work she does whether it is to earn a pay or to serve the Lord. She knows that nothing in life works like work itself.

So work is man's mandate from the Garden of Eden to eternity, and the Bible is clear that blessings only rest on the diligent not the indolent.

Distinction is borne out of dedication, not out of talk.

Talk is cheap, dedication is costly.

A wise woman will attend to the calling God has placed upon her life and produce that which honours His Name. Enduring the pain and standing the challenges it may require to produce what is a proof of the assignment upon her life without acting beyond the level of authority placed upon her in her home.

If the family must have more income in order to live a relatively comfortable life, it is not the time to justify your stay at home listening to tapes all day. The Kingdom of God has no hiding place for the lazy:

Go to the ant, thou sluggard; consider her ways, and be wise: Which having no guide, overseer, or ruler, Provideth her meat in the summer, and gathereth her food in the harvest. How long wilt thou sleep, O sluggard? when wilt thou arise out of thy sleep?

*Yet a little sleep, a little slumber, a little folding of the hands
to sleep: So shall thy poverty come as one that travelleth,
and thy want as an armed man.*
Proverbs 6:6-11 (KJV)

Godly women commit themselves to speaking in a godly way.

Then she fell on her face, and bowed herself to the ground, and said unto him, Why have I found grace in thine eyes, that thou shouldest take knowledge of me, seeing I am a stranger?
Ruth 2:10 (KJV)

The words of a person are a mirror of who they are. Out of the abundance of the heart the mouth speaks. Even what are considered as Freudian slips may not quite be, but a true mirror of what is on the heart.

We are surrounded today by people who use vulgar and unclean language. A lot of women are caught in the web of the same.

How does a godly woman respond knowing also that she must speak, after all she wants to express her self? The scriptures also teaches us that her words must be seasoned with grace; her words must be wholesome: We must not let corrupt communication come out of our mouth but only that which is profitable to the hearers.

We are told to build other people by our words. A godly woman knows what impact her words could have, either on her spouse if married, on her children or people around her. Therefore she qualifies who hears her, and what they hear from her.

A godly woman is totally dependent on God.

The LORD recompense thy work, and a full reward be given thee of the LORD God of Israel, under whose wings thou art come to trust.
Ruth 2:12 (KJV)

The people around you are conduits through which God will provide, produce or execute a promise. Your attitude must show trust in Him.

Trust in the LORD with all thine heart; and lean not unto thine own understanding.
In all thy ways acknowledge him, and he shall direct thy paths.
Proverbs 3:5-6 (KJV)

God is your shield, horn, salvation, and high tower.

The God of my rock; in him will I trust: he is my shield, and the horn of my salvation, my high tower, and my refuge, my saviour; thou savest me from violence.
2 Samuel 22:3 (KJV)

Be totally in love with the Lord and He will fill you with love.

But let all those that put their trust in thee rejoice: let them ever shout for joy, because thou defendest them: let them also that love thy name be joyful in thee.
Psalms 5:11 (KJV)

Confess that you will not be put to shame and He will make it happen for you.

O my God, I trust in thee: let me not be ashamed, let not mine enemies triumph over me.
Psalms 25:2 (KJV)

Declare that you will not be desolate, and He will make it your sweet experience.

Evil shall slay the wicked: and they that hate the righteous shall be desolate.
The LORD redeemeth the soul of his servants: and none of them that trust in him shall be desolate.
Psalms 34: 22 (KJV)

Always remember that men will fail you, if you put your confidence in them.

It is better to trust in the LORD than to put confidence in man. It is better to trust in the LORD than to put confidence in princes.
Psalms 118:8-9 (KJV)

Depend on God, know that not one of His Words will ever fail you.

God is not a man, that he should lie; neither the son of man,
that he should repent: hath he said, and shall he not do it? or
hath he spoken, and shall he not make it good?
Numbers 23:19 (KJV)

She knows that her dressing sends out a message.

Wash thyself therefore, and anoint thee, and put thy raiment upon thee, and get thee down to the floor: but make not thyself known unto the man, until he shall have done eating and drinking.
Ruth 3:3 (KJV)

She maketh herself coverings of tapestry; her clothing is silk and purple.
Proverbs 31:22 (KJV)

We said earlier in the book that a godly woman knows when to say no, to the desires of a man who tries to use you to express his own passions or perversions.

Remember that you are a walking Bible and a testimony to the glory of God. Everything you do must be for His honour, therefore if your clothing will bring disrepute to His Name, remember at all times that God has your best on His mind, therefore carry yourself in a way that honours His Name.

She is graced with a gift of discretion.

And she went down unto the floor, and did according to all that her mother in law bade her.

And when Boaz had eaten and drunk, and his heart was merry, he went to lie down at the end of the heap of corn: and she came softly, and uncovered his feet, and laid her down. And it came to pass at midnight, that the man was afraid, and turned himself: and, behold, a woman lay at his feet.

And he said, Who art thou? And she answered, I am Ruth thine handmaid: spread therefore thy skirt over thine handmaid; for thou art a near kinsman.

And he said, Blessed be thou of the LORD, my daughter: for thou hast shewed more kindness in the latter end than at the beginning, inasmuch as thou followedst not young men, whether poor or rich.

And now, my daughter, fear not; I will do to thee all that thou requirest: for all the city of my people doth know that thou art a virtuous woman.

And now it is true that I am thy near kinsman: howbeit there is a kinsman nearer than I.

Tarry this night, and it shall be in the morning, that if he will perform unto thee the part of a kinsman, well; let him do the kinsman's part: but if he will not do the part of a kinsman to thee, then will I do the part of a kinsman to thee, as the LORD liveth: lie down until the morning.

Ruth 3:6-13 (KJV)

Men and women have different abilities on matters of discernment and discretion. Ruth recognised the way to attract the attention of Boaz. She recognised that diligence was attractive to him, that humility got his attention. Ruth took note that to stand out in the presence of Boaz you could not overlook the way you dressed.

She recognised also that speech mattered to Boaz, not just the volume of what was said, but the content and the style in which it was said. A godly woman has the ability to interpret situations and know what is appropriate a response for each one.

Do not be carried away by the influence and opinion of friends which are a general and a blanket approach to all situations and matters. Remember you are called and graced with a gift of discretion and discernment. Use it, it will save you and protect you from dangerous situations. It will open doors for you where others have found frustration.

When wisdom entereth into thine heart, and knowledge is
pleasant unto thy soul;
Discretion shall preserve thee, understanding shall keep thee:
Proverbs 2:10-11 (KJV)

She knew greatness when she saw it in both Naomi and Boaz.

Appreciate greatness, recognise it, and not overlook it wherever you see it. It may be in the secular person: Because the person does not share your faith does not mean you cannot learn from what they have.

Eat the grapes and throw away the seed.

Take what they have, and reject what is unrighteous about it. Learn from other women who have been outstanding in the career you desire to pursue.

Learn from other women who have learned to take care of their physical body, and have particularly looked good to you. Without having to be vulgar, you can learn from the people who are around you.

Ruth saw what was outstanding about Naomi even in the midst of the tears and the cries.

She also recognised the power, strength, and respect Boaz controlled in the back woods of Bethlehem.

What you recognise is what works for you.

One of the marks of greatness is people who are unmarred or who have refused to be battered by all the human experience they have had. You have something to learn from them.

You might recognise it in your son or daughter who has potential for the future. Next time a great person comes around, respect what they have you will catch it like a magnet.

She listened to someone more knowledgeable than herself.

What you hear shapes you; what you hear determines who you become; what you hear focuses your sight.

Sight and sound direct life.

Sight and sound prepare you for victory.

The law of sound says "what you hear affects what you see, and becomes what you get".

Verily, verily, I say unto you, The hour is coming, and now is, when the dead shall hear the voice of the Son of God: and they that hear shall live.
John 5:25 (KJV)

Ruth chose to listen to her mother-in-law because she has been and seen the future before her. If you listen to fellow protégés, your colleagues, or players on the same football team, they will only describe your present position. Experience cannot be accelerated, bought, transferred or taught.

If you listen to those you call mentors they will paint
a picture of where you are going. Their painting is
not always easy, and their demand is often tough,
but if you must be somebody and go somewhere,
you must not listen to the praise of your colleagues,
but to the challenges of your mentors.

Godly women know they are the answer to someone's prayer.

The single woman who has not had an invitation out to dinner, who has not seen anyone, who has not heard any invitation, who has not been dated may feel sometimes that they are all alone, a mistake, and unwanted.

Carry yourself differently as a godly woman. Know and realise that if you desire to marry, you are the answer to somebody's prayer. Someone somewhere is waiting for you, and it is only a matter of time before what was faith will become sight.

So for the moment do not focus on the challenges around you, but on the solution which already exists in the spirit realm.

For our light affliction, which is but for a moment, worketh for us a far more exceeding and eternal weight of glory; While we look not at the things which are seen, but at the things which are not seen: for the things which are seen are temporal; but the things which are not seen are eternal.
2 Corinthians 4:17-18 (KJV)